BIBLE STORIES
YOU CAN'T FORGET
No Matter How Hard You Try

Marshall Efron & Alfa-Betty Olsen

illustrated by Ron Barrett

In the beginning of this book were two writers who, in the course of doing a television show on religion for children, discovered the King James Version of the Bible. They decided that it was (among 15 other things listed in their foreword): 1. A good source for good stories   2. Fun   3. Family entertainment.   11. Habit-forming.

As writers they felt the need to share this wonderful discovery. And what better way than to retell some of the stories with their own very contemporary wit and dramatic sense?

The television program was praised by such groups as the National Council of Churches and Action for Children's Television. Then came this book, with the retellings directed to readers (especially readers aloud) rather than viewers. Ron Barrett added his own dimension of finely drawn and intricate amusement.

Here, then, are eight stories, from the Old and New Testaments, to be read, shared, enjoyed in the spirit with which they were written—pleasure and respect.

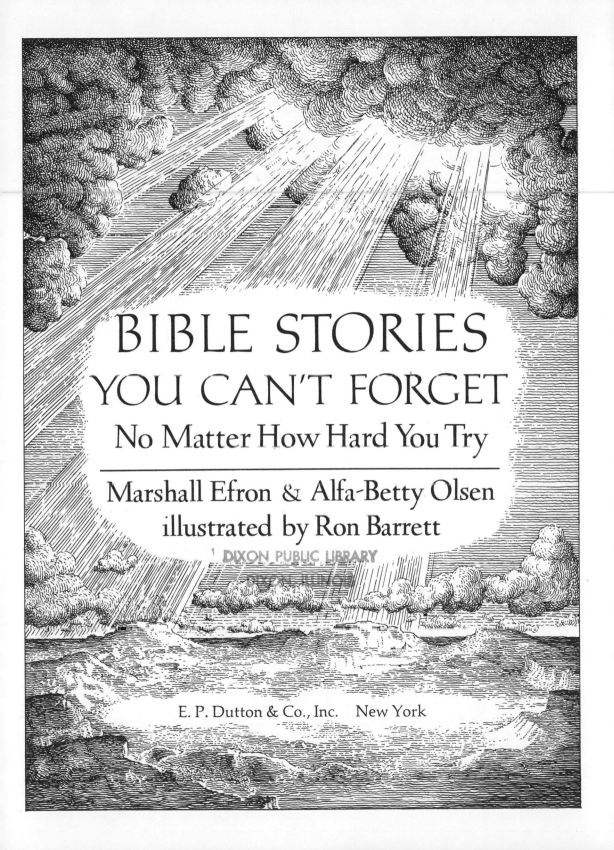

BIBLE STORIES
YOU CAN'T FORGET
No Matter How Hard You Try

Marshall Efron & Alfa-Betty Olsen
illustrated by Ron Barrett

E. P. Dutton & Co., Inc.   New York

Library of Congress Cataloging in Publication Data

Efron, Marshall
Bible stories you can't forget—no matter how hard you try

SUMMARY: Retelling of eight familiar Bible stories in
contemporary language.

1. Bible stories, English. [1. Bible stories]
I. Olsen, Alfa-Betty, joint author. II. Barrett, Ron.
III. Title

BS551.2.E26   220.9'505   76-9853   ISBN 0-525-26500-7

Published simultaneously in Canada by Clarke,
Irwin & Company Limited, Toronto and Vancouver

Designed by Riki Levinson
Printed in the U.S.A.   First Edition
10 9 8 7 6 5 4 3 2 1

To our respective parents
with much love

Foreword:
How This Book Came to Be

We think the Bible is:
1 A good source for good stories
2 Fun
3 Family entertainment
4 Mentioned a lot in a lot of good old books like *Moby Dick* or *The Scarlet Letter*
5 A best seller
6 Long
7 Available everywhere
8 A book full of questions
9 A book full of answers
10 A spiritual experience
11 Habit-forming
12 Good for you
13 A civilizing experience
14 Historical
15 An old book people still read, i.e., a classic.

And how did we find this out? How did two hard-boiled satirists (albeit with hearts of gold) discover that we felt this way? And why should we, two normal adults out to make a living, suddenly stop, drop everything, and concentrate upon the Bible? There's a story to be told here, and it goes like this:

A brave woman, named Pamela Ilot, head of the religion department at CBS, had lunch with our agent, the redoubtable Marian Searchinger. They put their heads together and the outcome was an offer for us to do one half-hour television show for children about religion and "it should be funny."

"You can do anything you want," Marian explained.

"Good," said Mr. Efron. "Let them tell us what to do and we'll do it."

"No, no, you don't understand. You get to be creative. You get to make it all up. The whole thirty minutes. Format. Concept. Content. All the words, all the actions. You'll love it!" Marian insisted.

"Great," said Mr. Efron. "I get to do what I've always wanted to do."

"What's that?" asked Miss Olsen, dubiously.

"I don't know," said Mr. Efron, brightly.

"Exactly what I suspected," said Miss Olsen.

Several weeks later, as we sat around wasting valuable time reading old patent medicine ads in the back pages of some old magazines Mr. Efron had pulled out of the garbage—Dr. Beaty's Ideal, Superior, Remarkable, Curative, and Efficacious Nerve Tonic: "Astounding Results Guaranteed!"—the title came to them. "We'll call it Marshall Efron's Illustrated, Simplified, and Painless Sunday School!"

"Terrific," said Mr. Efron. "But what's the show about?"

"What do you do in Sunday School?" asked Miss Olsen.

"Study Bible stories," answered Mr. Efron.

"Precisely, Dr. Efron," said Miss Olsen. "We'll tell Bible stories. You'll act them out."

"I'll use props," said Mr. Efron, dancing around the room. "I'll use toys, kitchen utensils—eggbeaters, cookie cutters—and . . . and what?"

"Costumes," said Miss Olsen, leading him into a waltz. "And wigs."

The show grew from one to ten and then some. They were very well received by everyone: the folks from CBS and the folks out there in America, ages three to eighty-three. We loved doing them and we loved our gang: Ted Holmes, our gentle and sympathetic producer; Alvin Thaler, our ebullient and energetic director; John Ward, who designed such wonderful sets. And Bill Leonard, a vice president at CBS, who was very supportive. But we loved the most, and owed the most to, King James I, and all we can say is, God Save the King.

These stories grow out of the television show scripts. Of course, since those scripts were written to be performed in front of the cameras and the stories in this book are meant to be read, we have rewritten, deleted, and added material.

For the most part, despite jokes and anachronisms, we have remained faithful to the King James Version. Occasionally we have had recourse to other translations and sources for amplification and clarification. That's how we got the names Balthazar, Melchior, and Gaspar in the story of The Three Wise Men. They are not named in the King James Bible.

We've taken great pleasure in discovering details in the stories that are not usually stressed: the fact that Noah was 600 years old when God asked him to build the Ark; that the rainbow appears in the sky as a token that never again will God destroy the world by flooding it; and the fact that Samson had to have been very hairy, indeed, since his hair had *never* been cut and here he was a grown man.

If we have any bias, it's toward human nature. We're against it.

And before we finish our Foreword, we'd also like to thank Ann Durell, our editor, for her patience and her eagle eye.

And now, friends, we give you our big book of bloodcurdling, electrifying, and recommended Bible stories—*Bible Stories You Can't Forget—No Matter How Hard You Try.*

Contents

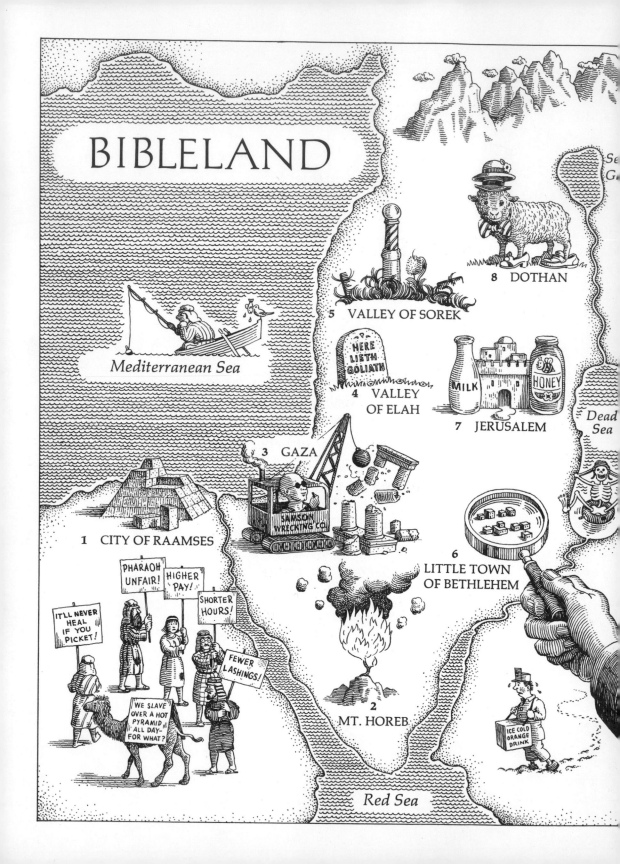

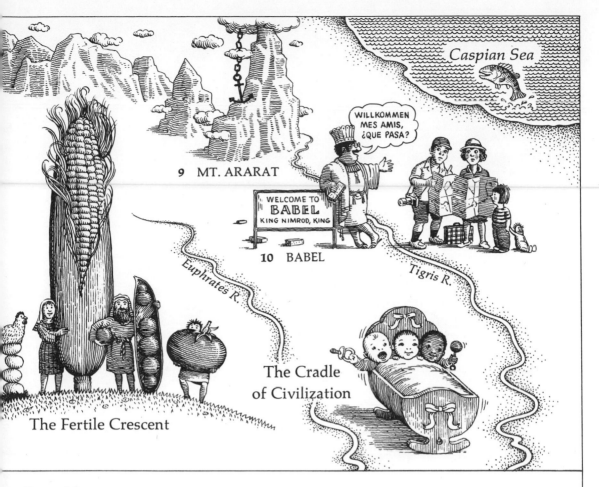

Caspian Sea

WILLKOMMEN MES AMIS, ¿QUE PASA?

9 MT. ARARAT

WELCOME TO
BABEL
KING NIMROD, KING

10 BABEL

Euphrates R.

Tigris R.

The Cradle
of Civilization

The Fertile Crescent

Key to Map

1 CITY OF RAAMSES Became famous when labor dispute between Pharaoh and labor leader Moses caused Moses to take slave-workers off the job. City now famous for unfinished pyramid.

2 MT. HOREB Home of the Burning Bush which delivered God's message to Moses. Today burning bushes are extinct.

3 GAZA Where Samson pulled down the great temple. The town has never been the same.

4 VALLEY OF ELAH Where David slew Goliath. Backwards Elah reads hale, as in hale and hearty, which David had to be to take on Goliath, also a hale fellow, albeit a bit backwards.

5 VALLEY OF SOREK Home of Delilah. Also known as a clip joint.

6 LITTLE TOWN OF BETHLEHEM Birthplace of Lord Baby Jesus and site of astronomical phenomenon late one December, nearly 2,000 years ago.

7 JERUSALEM Capital city of the Land of Milk and Honey. Home of King Herod. And what better location for the home of a king, than a capital.

8 DOTHAN Where Joseph's brothers brought their sheep to graze, and where they sold Joseph to the Bedouin traders. If you go there, don't wear your best clothing.

9 MT. ARARAT Where Noah's Ark landed after the Flood. While we have no trouble locating Mt. Ararat, no one has found the Ark yet. Keep looking, it has to be there, somewhere.

10 BABEL Home of King Nimrod, site of famous tower, and the great hotbed of languages.

Noah's Ark

The story of Noah can be found in the Book of Genesis; it begins in Chapter 6. It takes place early in the Old Testament and in the story of Man. Mankind hadn't lived long on the earth, but already everyone was very evil and very violent. These were terrible times.

When two people met did they shake hands? No. They raised their fists at one another, curled their lips back, bared their teeth, and growled.

And when your average citizen went to a restaurant, he'd wear his hat and coat the whole time, because if he hung them up, they'd be stolen.

Also, no one ever ate anything cooked.

And God saw this and had regrets. Big regrets. Creator's regrets. He was sorry the world had turned out so badly and he decided he was going to wipe it all out with a big Flood and start all over again. He was going to wipe man and beast and creeping things and birds right off the face of the earth. It was going to be a big-time erasure.

However, there was one man who found grace in the eyes of the Lord, the only good man on earth, Old Noah. And God planned to spare him and his family.

At this time Noah was 600 years old, and that means he had been an old man already for 530 years. Way, way back in Genesis people lived to be very old. You know how they say, "As old as Methuselah"? Well, Methuselah, according to the Book of Genesis, lived for 969 years. And that's old. Noah lived to be pretty old too. He lived to be 950 years old. Nobody knows how he did it, there's just no way to account for it.

When God decided to tell Noah about His plans, God cast His eye over the world and found Noah right in front of his own house, bent over, clutching his knobby old knee and singing, "Soon it's gonna rain, I can feel it."

And while he was standing that way, he noticed some crumpled beer cans, soda pop bottles, cigarette butts, and a broken comb in the gutter, so he picked them up and put them in the trash basket.

"Every litter bit hurts, and how," he said. "It's hard to bend when you're 600 years old and, you know what? It's harder to straighten up."

Then God spoke, "Noah!" He said, "I want you to build a boat."

"You want me to build a boat?" Noah asked. "You should have asked me 580 years ago."

"You want me to build a boat?" Noah asked.
"You should have asked me 580 years ago."

"Noah," God continued, "the end is coming. There's too much evil here. I'm going to destroy the earth. I'm going to send a great Flood. Build an Ark and make it according to these specifications: first, make it of cypress wood, 450 feet long, 75 feet wide, and 45 feet high. Second, I want three decks, a door in the side, and a window under the eaves. And take your family into it and take two of every animal and bird and creeping thing into it and take enough food for all of you to eat. That way you'll survive."

"Okay, if you say so, Lord, I'll do it," Noah told him.

And God added, "And hurry. Soon it's gonna rain."

"Yes, sir, like a shot," said Noah as he shuffled off, just as fast as his two little old feet would carry him.

Now Noah had three sons—Ham, Shem, and Japheth—they were the sons of his middle age and that made them about 100 years old at this time. They were good old boys, so when Noah told them about God's command, they all pitched in and went to work . . . like a shot.

And Mrs. Noah, Mrs. Ham, Mrs. Shem, and Mrs. Japheth worked right along with them. It was a family affair.

They ripped, they sawed, they hammered, they glued, they painted, they pitched, they varnished, they lacquered, they caulked. In a word, they built a boat.

The four old men, climbing up and down ladders, scrambling over the sides of the boat, moving massive timbers around were a spectacular sight to behold. And people came from all over to see it and laugh and mock and make fun of them.

"Hey," said one. "Look at Noah's folly!"

"Soon it's gonna rain," answered Noah.

"There's no fool like an old Noah," said another.

"Soon it's gonna rain," replied Shem.

"You'll be drinking those words," added Japheth.

"He's not in his second childhood, he's in his fiftieth!" somebody else called out to them.

"Soon it's gonna rain," answered Ham.

"You're laughing now," added Noah, "but he who laughs last laughs best, and he who laughs now is gonna choke on salty tears later on."

"You'll never get it off the ground," yelled a man from the back of the crowd.

"Soon it's gonna rain," Noah yelled back, and felt a twinge in his knee and went on working.

Noah had only seven days to build the Ark, get the animals on board, load up enough food for everyone, and batten down the hatches before the rains would come. There was so much to do, and not enough time to do it in, that Noah could be heard giving orders late into the night:

"Tote that barge. Lift that burro!"

"Watch out for the armadillos!"

"Get those mosquitoes on board. You know God made them so we could appreciate the flies!"

"And put the bats in the belfry!"

Noah put on the Ark a pair of every animal. We would like to mention who they were, but it would take too much time. *They* know who they are, and *you* know who they are, and *we'd* rather not risk leaving someone out and hurting his, hers, or its feelings.

After all the animals and all the food was on board, there

was nothing else to do but for Noah, his wife, his three sons, and their wives to get aboard. And they did. And they battened down the hatches and God sealed the Ark and then. . .

It started to rain.

And it rained and it rained and it rained.

It rained for forty days and forty nights.

And it rained and it rained and it rained.

And the Flood was upon the Earth.

And it rained and it rained and it rained.

And the water covered the hills and it rained and it rained and it rained.

And the water covered the mountains.

And every living thing under the Flood perished, except the fish.

But every living thing above the Flood, everybody who was in the Ark, Noah and his family and every animal and bird and creeping thing were all snug and dry and the bugs in the rugs were too.

And then the rain stopped. They couldn't hear it beat on the roof anymore. They couldn't see it beat on the window anymore. So Noah stepped outside on the deck to see what he could see. What he saw was a big, big Flood. And everything was dripping wet. And water was falling on him from the roof.

"Water, water everywhere. You step outside, you wet your hair," he said.

Up ahead the top of a mountain was beginning to show above the level of the water. Noah got all excited. He jumped up and down and beat his sides.

And the dove flew off and returned that evening
bearing an olive branch in his beak.

"Look, Ma," he said to Mrs. Noah. "Look, Ma, top of the world! The Flood is going. It's over. It's over."

And everybody came tumbling out onto the deck. Mr. and Mrs. Ham, Mr. and Mrs. Shem, and Mr. and Mrs. Japheth.

"But where is the dry land? All we see is water," they said.

"Funny you should ask," said Noah. "I have an idea. Bring me a dove. Bring me Donald Dove. He's dependable."

So Ham went back and found Donald Dove and brought him to Noah.

"Donald Dove," Noah said, "I want to talk to you. I have a mission for you. Go out and find out if the world is dry enough for us to get off this Ark."

And the dove flew off and returned that evening bearing an olive branch in his beak.

"Ahh, Donald, welcome back," said Noah. "I see you turned over a new leaf. Okay, now, if the world is dry enough for you, go and don't come back." He released the dove and Donald flew up into the sky and was gone, never to be seen again.

Then Noah prayed, "Oh Lord, Lord, is it true? Can we leave the Ark?"

God answered, "Yes, Noah. Go forth from the Ark and take thy wife and thy sons and thy sons' wives. And bring forth with thee the animals and the birds and the creeping things. And all of you—be fruitful and multiply and replenish the Earth."

Noah asked God, "Will there ever be another flood like this one?"

God replied, "No, Noah. And as a demonstration of my

good will, I will set a sign in the clouds and you will call it a rainbow and you will take that as a token, my promise that the waters shall never again become a flood to destroy all living things."

Noah said, "Thank you, God."

Then he and his wife and his sons and their wives and all the animals disembarked and started the world all over again.

And Noah lived happily for 350 more years. And when he finally died, he was 950 years old. Which is quite enough for anybody.

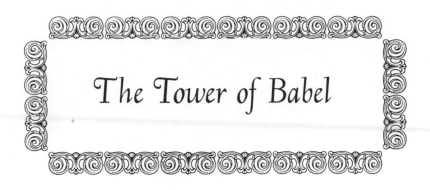

The Tower of Babel

The story of the Tower of Babel is about many stories, one on top of the other. It's about the first skyscraper or high-rise building ever. This story can be found in the Book of Genesis in the Old Testament, Chapters 10 and 11, and takes place way, way back sometime after the Great Flood, when everybody in the world spoke the same language and was the descendant of Noah.

It all happened in the city of Babel. Now, people who live in Paris are called Parisians; in Rome they're called Romans; in New York, New Yorkers; and in Babel they were called Babblers. This is important. Commit this to memory.

The city of Babel, in its heyday, was a major league city and was ruled over by a celebrated king, whose name was Nimrod. He was a mighty hunter and a man who really loved himself. In fact, he was his own favorite person.

Every year on his birthday Nimrod made a speech, the same speech, but this year it was different. This year he had something to say. It started out as usual.

"Hello. I'm Nimrod. Let me tell you about myself. I've had an extraordinary life. You'll find it fascinating. When I was nine months old I started to walk. Isn't that wonderful? And when I was a year old I was speaking. Incredible! In the beginning there wasn't much I could say— 'Mama, Papa, cookie, gimmeeee, gimmeeee, mine, mine, mine.' I was a darling baby. By the time I was six, I was ready for the first grade. I bet you're impressed. And on my twenty-first birthday I killed my first bore. That was Uncle Charlie. And now here I am, the ruler of the kingdom. And we're the hottest thing around!"

His people were starting to fall asleep. They'd heard all of this before—many times. One man was even heard to say, "This is the bunk," just before he drifted off to dreamland.

But then Nimrod came to the part of his speech which was new and which had never been said before, and woke everybody up.

"We've just recently had a big breakthrough," he announced. "Scientists in our labs have come up with this! The Brick!"

He held up a brick for everyone to see.

"Look," he shouted, "no moving parts! Small, handy, portable, durable, can withstand the effects of time, every one the same shape, the same size, *and* they fit together. Let me show you in this demonstration."

He took five rocks and tried to pile them up neatly. The best he could do was something that looked like a sloppy pyramid. Then he took five bricks and stacked them one on top of the other. In a matter of seconds. Everyone was impressed.

"You see," he explained, "this is revolutionary. We've revolutionized the construction industry."

The people of Babel cheered. Nimrod stopped them. He had more to say. "With this invention, we can rule the world. There's no end to its uses. It has unlimited possibilities. It's something to build on. Yes. I can really build something big with this. Wait a minute!" he suddenly exclaimed. "I'm getting an idea." His eyes glowed. "Hold on," he cried out. "I'm having a hubris attack!" (A hubris attack is when you get filled up with pride and think you can do anything and anything you think you can do, you do.) Nimrod stood up. "I'm going to build a stairway to the stars," he shouted. "It'll reach heaven and I can visit God. The sky's the limit!"

He sprang into action. "Architects," he ordered, "draw those plans! Workers, make those bricks! Everybody get to work!"

And they did. The work went on for weeks and then for months. Nimrod visited the construction site every day and sang, "I'll Build a Stairway to Paradise," to the workers. And gave them pep talks: "Remember, Babel is number one. This tower will be bigger and better than anything *God* ever made."

The brick factories worked overtime, and the tower grew larger and larger and larger until it touched the clouds—and still the workers of Babel kept building. And Nimrod's head was growing too. It was growing larger and larger and his thoughts were in the clouds.

"You see," he explained, "this is revolutionary.
We've revolutionized the construction industry."

I'll bet God will be surprised to see me up there in His presence, Nimrod thought. I'll bet He'll be mightily impressed. He'll probably want to ask my advice about things. Well, I'll be glad to give it to Him. But for some things He'll have to pay.

God didn't like this. What He said was, "That takes the cake. And besides, this building is breaking my zoning laws. This building is a brick blight. I'll have to put out that blight. They're building this tower to challenge me, not to praise me. It's the wrong attitude. I'm going to have to teach them a lesson. I'm going to confound their language so they cannot understand one another's speech."

From then on strange things began to happen. One worker, who was building a pediment and singing, "I'll Build a Stairway to the Stars," turned to a fellow worker and said, "Hand me that wacknum."

"What?" said the fellow worker.

The first worker said, "*Please* hand me that wacknum."

"Wacknum?" said the second worker.

"That frunkin, the fornash," said the first worker, getting irritated.

The second worker was now himself affected by the strange spell and what he said was, "Cornish hamah vorbebe?"

Which got the first worker all worked up. In fact, he was beside himself with rage. Shaking his fists in the air, he shouted, "Haknah, naruba, you muttonhead!"

Worker number two threw a brick at him, shouting, "Call me a muttonhead, will you? Dak friganook!"

But the brick sailed past its intended mark and struck another worker, who was working two stories down, causing a great lump to spring up on his forehead.

"Who did that?" he shouted. "Who hit me with a peachface?"

"I'll peachface you in a minute," said a hod carrier, who was working nearby, and he threw a few more bricks all over the place.

Within a matter of minutes fights were springing up everywhere on the tower. Workers were becoming irritated, impatient, and angry with one another, and nobody could understand anybody. The work stopped as they went after each other with their tools. There were some hair-raising chases.

One man, who was trying to make peace, stood on a platform, raised his arms, and addressed the general brawl. "Boys! Boys! Listen to me."

They did. They stopped and gave him their attention. And this is what he said: "Hinky, pinky! Wincky, wincky! Do wah doo wah do."

This started the fighting all over again. And as the men fought, parts of the tower became unglued and it started to crumble. The workers continued to fight and the tower continued to crumble. And still they continued to fight. Things were getting shaky.

Large pieces of the tower broke off and rolled and tumbled in the air and crashed to the earth far below. People on the ground, the citizens of Babel, cried out, "Oh my goodness, the tower is collapsed. Run for your parpin!"

One woman shouted, "Mercer arts! Mercer arts!"

Within a matter of minutes fights were springing up
everywhere on the tower.

And another yelled, "La tour esta verstoren."

No one could understand anyone else and there came a roar and a huge shower of bricks and dust and workers and noise, and nobody could see anything and the day became like night because the dust hung in the air like a great big curtain. The whole tower was pulverized into dust, and when the dust cleared and settled and covered everything, all that remained were five broken bricks that looked like a sloppy pyramid.

When Nimrod came and took a look at it, all he could say was, "Well, back to the old dworking borkman."

Nobody could understand him. Nobody could understand anybody else either.

Men who'd been friends for years couldn't understand each other.

And women who'd been friends for years couldn't understand each other.

Husbands and wives couldn't understand each other.

Children couldn't understand each other.

In short, nobody knew nothing.

The people of Babel had finally earned the name Babblers.

They all left and went off in different directions and founded new languages, and that is how the people of the world came to speak so many languages.

Joseph and the
Coat of Many Colors

Joseph and the Coat of Many Colors is a story of intrigue and anger and hatred and grief and love and corruption and buying and selling and rending of garments and jealousy and weeping and wailing and gnashing of teeth, of rage and fear and misery and heartbreak, and it is ultimately a story of chickens coming home to roost. It's found in the Old Testament, the Book of Genesis, Chapter 37.

It starts with an old man, Jacob, who had many sons. One of them, Joseph, was his favorite. Joseph was born when Jacob was already an old man and Jacob loved to watch him grow.

Jacob coddled Joseph and bored everybody with stories about how good Joseph was:

"Joseph made his bed today."

"Joseph carried his dish to the sink all by himself, without anybody having to ask him."

The most beautiful coat in the world.

"Joseph didn't spill his milk."

"Joseph saw his shadow and didn't get scared."

Now Joseph was seventeen years old when our story takes place. And he had eleven older brothers, who resented him fiercely.

"Somehow you just can't warm up to Joseph, he's so good," said one.

"Ditto," said another.

"I'll second that emotion," said a third.

"You've got my vote," said a fourth.

"Mine, too," said fifth and sixth.

"You can count me in," said the seventh.

"I'll drink to that," said the eighth.

"I'll eat to that," said the ninth.

"You ain't just a' whistlin' Dixie," said the tenth.

"So what else is new?" said the eleventh.

In a word, they agreed, "Joseph is a schmo."

Then one day, Jacob called Joseph into his tent. He had a package.

"Joseph," he said, holding out the gift, "here's a present for you on You Day—a day to celebrate that you are you. Happy you to you. A truly unique personality. Open it up. Open the package!"

Jacob held out a large white box to Joseph, who took it, opened it, and removed what was inside. He held it up and his eyes grew large, his jaw dropped. It was the most beautiful thing he had ever seen. The most beautiful coat in the world!

The front represented a gorgeous sunrise with bright yellows and reds dancing in between shimmering greens and pinks and bright stones glittering in all of the rainbow colors.

The shoulders of the coat dripped a lovely rich orange—a cross between tangerine and pumpkin and persimmon and carrot, so no matter how you sliced it, it was a funny orange.

The back of the coat was a desert sunset full of rich reds, and blues and purples and deep grays shaded with lavender.

The sleeves glowed in iridescent candy colors of cream, chocolate brown, peppermint red-and-white, lime green, and cherry red.

And the lining was composed of glowing gold and silver satin.

All in all, a veritable humdinger. Joseph's eyes were stunned with the colors.

Remember this coat. Remember it well. How could you forget it? It adds color to our story. Many of them. And it is the cause of lots of grief, because Joseph's brothers were very jealous, and grumbled amongst themselves. The envy of Joseph's brothers added another color to our story—green! There's hunter green and celery green and parrot green, but this was jealousy green.

Another thing about Joseph was that Joseph was a dreamer. In those days dreams were considered messages from the Lord. And Joseph had two dreams, which he told to everybody one night at dinner.

"I dreamt," he began, "that me, and you, my brothers, were in the field tying our sheaves of grain and when we had tied our sheaves, all of your sheaves arranged themselves in a circle around my sheaf and bowed down to it."

The brothers shuddered and said to each other, "Ohhhhhhh, I hate him. Bow down to him? That'll be the day. Oh boy, is he in love with himself."

And then Joseph said, "Just to prove how great I am, let me tell you my second dream. You do want to hear it, don't you?"

And Jacob said, "We all want to hear it, don't we, boys?"

There was a great deal of silence, which emanated from the boys.

So Jacob repeated himself. "We all want to hear it, don't we, boys?"

"No, no, no, no, no, no, no," said the boys.

But Jacob said, "Go ahead, Joseph. I'd like to hear it. It's fascinating. Joseph, everything you say is fascinating."

One of the brothers said, under his breath, "I'd rather go outside and watch my fingernails grow." And the others agreed with him. But before they could leave, Joseph told his dream anyway, and it went like this:

"The sun and the moon and eleven stars bowed down to me. The sun and the moon are my parents and the eleven stars are you, my brothers."

"That's quite enough, Joseph," said Jacob, his parent. "I'm sorry I heard that."

The brothers were sorry they heard it too. Sorry and not a little bit angry. They all leapt up immediately with the intention of running out of the house, which is exactly what they did. Anything to get away from Joseph.

Bear in mind that Joseph couldn't help what he dreamed and that the dreams were messages from God. But his brothers didn't want to hear about it. They waxed wroth. (Later Roth

[23]

came in and waxed them. But that's a horse of a different feather.) Anyway, the brothers were so wroth that when Jacob's sheep had eaten all the grass in Jacob's fields, they were happy and eager to take the sheep and go looking for greener pastures, and to put as much distance between themselves and Joseph as they could.

They left.

A few hours later, Jacob began to worry about them.

"Joseph, Joseph, Joseph, light of my life, fire of my heart, come here," he cried.

"What? What do you want?" said Joseph, coming into his father's tent.

"I want you to take a little trip," said Jacob. "See what your brothers are doing. Tell me if they're going to get in any trouble, or do anything I don't like."

So Joseph went off to do his father's bidding and check up on his brothers.

Meanwhile, out in the fields, in the wilderness, the brothers were congratulating themselves on being away from Joseph.

"Ahhhhh, peace at long last. If I have to hear about Joseph's dreams one more time, I won't be responsible for what I do," they all said.

Then one of the brothers saw something coming towards them from far away. "Oh my goodness," he gasped, "do you see what I see?"

Somebody else said, "It's Joseph, come to spy on us."

And somebody else said, "And he's wearing that coat! Ohhhh, the schmendrick!"

Then they conspired amongst themselves to kill him. They were simple men, you see, and didn't know any better. It hadn't occurred to them that there were less drastic measures.

"Let us kill him and cast him into that old pit over there and we'll say some wild beast did it," suggested the fiercest of the brothers. The others all concurred except for one, who was more reasonable than the rest. That was Reuben (he was named after the sandwich), and he said, "Include me out."

Reuben went on to explain, "I don't like him either, but after all, he is our brother. You don't want to be a brother-slayer. Just throw him into the pit. And we'll figure out something else later."

Reuben planned to come later, when it was dark, and free Joseph.

That was as far as they got with the conversation because Joseph was almost within hearing distance. "Quiet, here he comes," said the brothers.

Joseph's first words to his brothers were, "Hi, guys. Hello, my brothers. Joseph's brothers. How are you?"

They immediately seized him and stripped him of his coat. And threw him into the pit.

Joseph's last words to his brothers were, "What have I done to offend you?"

It was terrible down in the pit. Dark, dry, no water, no food, and no way out. Poor Joseph, trapped and alone. Joseph said, "I think I'll call this the Pit of Despair."

Meanwhile, Reuben decided to lure the brothers away. He said, "Let us go off and look for richer pastures."

But the brothers foxed him. "Why don't *you* go look? When *you* find it, we'll follow."

So Reuben was in a bind and had to do it. If he didn't, he ran the risk of arousing their suspicions.

He left.

While he was gone, and the brothers were sitting down to their lunch, a caravan of traders passed nearby and stopped. And Judah, another of the brothers, got an idea. "There's no profit in killing Joseph. After all, he is our brother, he is our flesh and blood. We don't want to have his blood on our hands. And if we sell him to those merchants over there, there *is* a profit," he argued.

The other brothers heartily concurred. "That's right. We'll get rid of Joe and make some Jack to boot," they said and laughed.

And that's what they did, the cruel, unfeeling brothers. The creepies. They got twenty pieces of silver for him, and poor Joseph went off with the caravan—sold as a slave.

The brothers felt really pleased with themselves, until Reuben returned and looked into the pit.

"Where is Joseph? I looked in the pit and he wasn't there," said Reuben.

"We sold him," said the brothers. "Here's your share."

"But what will we tell our father, you twits?" said Reuben.

"Ohhhhhh," said the brothers. "We hadn't thought of that." And then they thought about it until one of them got an idea.

"You know what we can do?" he said. "We can kill a little goat and put his blood on the coat and bring it back to Jacob

And poor Joseph went off with the caravan—sold as a slave.

and tell him that Joseph met with an unfortunate accident. A wild beast ate him."

So the evil plotters smeared the coat with blood and brought it back to Jacob.

"We found this in the field," said the brothers.

Jacob believed them and his heart was broken. "Oh woe, oh woe, oh woe. Joseph, my favorite, my baby, the light of my life. Oh woe." And Jacob rended his clothes.

And Joseph, poor Joseph, what of Joseph? Joseph was sold again as a slave into Egypt. And crossed the burning sands and many bridges. We invite you to read the Book of Genesis for the continuing saga of Joseph, his dreams, other people's dreams, famine and fame and the chickens that come home to roost, and the justice that is lying in wait for Joseph's evil brothers.

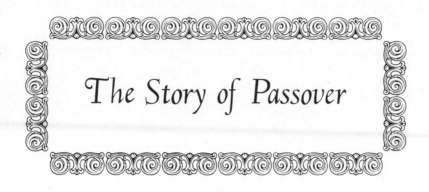

The Story of Passover

The story of Passover is found in the Book of Exodus in the Old Testament, Chapters 1 through 13—it's a longie.

It takes place in Egypt, the land of the Sphinx, the land of the Pyramids, and the land of the Pharaohs, and is the story of how the Children of Israel won their freedom from a tyrant and despot and were allowed to escape into the desert—a place where no one usually wants to go.

At the time our story begins, the people of Israel had been in Egypt for 430 years and, during that time, they had gone from riches to rags and become slaves to the Egyptian Pharaoh. There's not much to be said for being a slave. It's no fun unless you like to take orders and be abused, there's little room for advancement, and the wages you get are slave wages. Slave wages is chicken feed, peanuts, and that ain't hay.

And what were the slaves doing? What were they slaving at?

PHARAOHLAND, an amusement park that, as he put it,
"is gonna wow 'em for centuries."

Well, the answer to that is a strange one. They were in the real estate development industry. Egypt had a lot of property, and when you have a lot of property, what do you do with it? You build on it.

The man in charge of Egypt, the head honcho and the number one slave driver, was the Pharaoh. He was Emperor, King, Master-Builder and Chief-Contractor all rolled into one. As he put it, "I was born to build," and that's why he had BORN TO BUILD tattooed on the soft and flabby bicep of his left arm.

He thought of himself as a benefactor and visionary. "I have the ideas and the slaves do the sweating and straining. That makes me Mr. Wonderful and makes them tired. That also gives them all the muscles and I have this attractive fat all over my body."

He didn't like to walk any more than he liked to work. It wasn't dignified. Whenever he traveled, it was by camel.

And he didn't drive around on just an ordinary camel. That was because he was not an ordinary camel driver. His camel had three humps—it was a custom camel, and it came equipped with a glass partition between the first and the second humps, a built-in soda fountain, a sun roof, and its own telephone. It was called the XCL 2000—X for experimental, C for camel, and L for longer. The 2000 was what it cost to feed it every day.

Pharaoh was involved in a long-term, big-scale project which was going to take decades to finish: PHARAOHLAND, an amusement park that, as he put it, "is gonna wow 'em for centuries."

He had had signs installed all over the place: WATCH US GROW,

[31]

DIG WE MUST FOR A BETTER EGYPT, and OVERSEERS, TASKMASTERS, AND RULERS MUST WEAR HARD-HEARTS AT ALL TIMES.

That was Pharaoh: a man who could say about his slaves, the men who did the actual work on all his projects, "Ungrateful wretches! I've given them everything they have—the rags they wear, the lashes they bear. I wish they'd appreciate it!" a man who never worked at his desk, but spent all his time drinking brandy Alexander-the-Greats at business feasts. Yes, that was Pharaoh, one side of the story. Now for Moses, the other side.

At this time Moses lived far away in another country where he tended his father-in-law's flocks of sheep. He was a youthful eighty—bright, alert, a lot of spring in his step.

He was a man with a past—a special past—this man called Moses—and little did he know he had a special kind of future coming up.

He was born in Egypt during a time of great trouble for the Jews, and he was a Jew himself. It had been decreed that every newborn Jewish boy was to be killed—tossed into the Nile River as food for the crocodiles. But Moses' mother was shrewd and hid her baby in a watertight basket, like a small boat, and left the basket in the bullrushes in the river near where the Pharaoh's daughter bathed herself.

This Princess of the Nile, well-known as a clean woman, found the basket, adopted the baby Moses, and raised him as her own. So the Jewish baby was raised and educated in the Royal Court, the palace of his people's enemies.

He lived the life of an Egyptian aristocrat until one day, when he was forty years old, he came across an Egyptian overseer mistreating a Hebrew slave. Uncontrollable anger bubbled up inside him and he clobbered the Egyptian and buried him in the sand. (This is one of your early cover-ups. Adam and Eve were the first, when they donned fig leaves and denied everything.) Moses had to flee and that is how he wound up in Midian, where he was a shepherd for forty years. And since he was forty when he left Egypt, and forty years had passed since then, he was now eighty, but nimble.

One day he took the flocks to graze in the mountains above the desert, and as he was letting the sheep roam around and graze, an Angel of the Lord appeared to him in a flame of fire out of the midst of a bush.

Moses looked at this sight, amazed. "The bush burns," he exclaimed, "but is not consumed. This must be a miracle."

But then the deep, resonant, mysterious voice of God echoed through the air. "Moses," said the Lord, "this is God speaking. Remove your shoes. You are on holy ground."

So Moses took his sandals off.

After that God spoke again. "Moses, I am sending you on a mission. I have heard the groaning of the Children of Israel and I am going to deliver them out of the hands of the Egyptians and bring them to a Land of Milk and Honey called Canaan. I want you to represent me and go before them and tell them, "I AM THAT I AM HATH SENT YOU."

And Moses said, "That's cryptic, Lord. It occurs to me that they might listen to me, but what if they don't believe me? What if they say, 'The Lord never appeared to you'?"

"Take your staff and throw it on the ground," commanded God, in a very stern voice.

Moses did as he was told and when his staff touched the

ground, it turned into a wriggly, writhing, colorful snake.

"Ugh!" said Moses, backing away. "A snake. How yishy."

"Moses," said God, "put forth your hand and take it by the tail."

"You're not serious, Lord," said Moses. "I don't want to touch this snake. Can't you make it something soft and cuddly, like a hamster?"

God was in no mood for jokes. "Do as I say," He ordered.

So Moses took a deep breath and bent over and picked up the snake. "A snake it is, Lord," he said. But as soon as he touched it, the snake became his staff again. "Ahhh," said Moses, "a snake it was, a staff it is. That's a nifty miracle, Lord, but what if they still don't believe me?"

God said, "We will show them something to make them thoroughly frightened and then they will believe. Moses, put your hand inside your robe over your heart and then take it out . . . your hand."

Moses did so, and when he took his hand out and looked at it, he shuddered. It had turned white, like snow, a sickly, pale, leprous white. Moses wanted to faint.

God said, "They will believe that."

And Moses said, "I believe it. It's awful."

Then God said, "Okay now, put your hand back inside your robe."

And Moses put his hand into his robe again, and when he took it out, it was back to normal.

"Good as new," said the Lord. "Do that for the Children of Israel, but if they should need another sign, pour river water upon the ground and it will turn to blood."

"That's fine, Lord," said Moses, "but one more thing. I don't talk too good, no how."

And the Lord replied, "I see what you mean."

"I got what you call your lead tongue," Moses went on.

"That's enough!" said God. "I made your mouth as I made everybody's mouth, and I gave everyone speech as well as sight and hearing too. So trust me."

"Even so," said Moses, "I cannot make words come out good—especially in what you call your stress situation."

"This burns me," said God, "but here's the solution. You remember your brother, Aaron? Well, he's coming to visit you. We'll make him your spokesman. I'll tell you and you'll tell him. Is that fair?"

Moses bowed his head. "That's fine, Lord. I will do as you command. But tell me, what about Pharaoh, he's not going to let his slaves go."

"I was just getting to that," God answered. "You must go before Pharaoh and show him the signs I have given you, and you must say to him, 'Let my people go.' And his heart will be hard, but I will stretch out my hand and smite Egypt with my wonders and after that he will let my children go. And now, Moses, it's time for you to go."

And so Moses and his family left Midian. They linked up with Aaron out in the wilderness and together they all went to see the Children of Israel in the land of Egypt.

When they had assembled the Children of Israel before them, God told Moses and Moses told Aaron and Aaron told the crowd of God's plan. The elders in the crowd scratched their heads, murmured, mumbled, and didn't seem convinced. So Aaron demonstrated the staff-into-a-snake miracle, the leprous-hand miracle, and the water-into-blood miracle, which convinced everyone. Indeed, they were most impressed and started to pray.

The next step was to go before Pharaoh.

Moses said, "My God has commanded me to say unto you: 'Let my people go into the desert to worship me.' "

And Pharaoh laughed. "Who is this God that tells *me* what to do? *I* don't listen to anyone. *I* am Pharaoh and *I* need my slaves. There's a dispute here," he pointed out. "God calls them *His* people but I think of them as *My* people, and I am always right. Always have been, always will be. As for these slaves, if they have all this time to think about their God, they're not putting enough time in on the job. I'll give them something to keep them busy. I shall make their work harder. Henceforth they shall have to find their own straw to make bricks with. Put that in your pipe and smoke it."

And Pharaoh sent out orders to his straw bosses that the company would no longer supply straw to the Jewish slaves for the making of bricks, which made their job more difficult, if not impossible. Straw was necessary to help hold the brick mixture together.

The Jewish slaves soon had their hands full. They quickly used up the straw they had and had to look for more, but there was no more. They pulled up stubble from the earth and used that, but the stubble was soon used up. Brick production slowed. Finally brick production crumbled. The taskmasters grumbled. No one was happy.

Moses spoke to God. "Lord," he said, "I'm afraid I've made things worse for the Children of Israel. It's awful. No bricks, no work—just punishment. What do I do now?"

And God had an answer. "Go back to Pharaoh," he said, "and tell him again, 'Let my people go.' I will incite him to stubbornness and he will refuse to set Israel free. After that, I will perform miracles to convince the Egyptians that I AM God and then they will *drive* the Children of Israel from Egypt."

"Whatever you say, Lord," replied Moses, and he and Aaron went before Pharaoh again and a duel took place between Moses and Pharaoh's magicians. It was called, "Can You Top This?".

Moses threw Aaron's staff on the ground and it turned into a snake. But to Moses' surprise, the magicians did likewise.

So Moses turned the water of the Nile to blood. But to his amazement, the sneaky magicians also did likewise.

Moses was very depressed. He felt very bad and it didn't help when Pharaoh laughed at all of them (this Pharaoh was sometimes known as the laughing Pharaoh) and said, "These are silly tricks. Leave me alone. I'll never let my slaves go. I have things to build." And just as if to prove his point, at that moment a phone call came in from his chief architect, Edifis, who had a new monument he wanted to build.

"How long will it take to put up?" asked Pharaoh.

"Three centuries," said the architect.

"That's too long," said Pharaoh. "Cut it to two!" And he exited laughing.

God instructed Moses to go before Pharaoh again and Moses did. "I'm sorry, Pharaoh," he said, "but it's time to escalate. It's time for God to send His plagues upon the land of Egypt. It's time for the plague of frogs!"

God sent frogs out of the river and they covered the land. They were everywhere. They were in people's beds, their ovens, where they cooked, in the bowls where they ate. Uggghhhhh. It was awful.

And Pharaoh said, "Okay, okay, I'll let your people go. But get rid of these frogs." He wasn't laughing.

So all the frogs died and smelled bad. But dead frogs were better than a plague of frogs, and Pharaoh changed his mind.

"I changed my mind," he told the Jews. "Get back to work. Tote that barge. Lift that bale. You know the old cliché." And he was back to laughing again.

"Okay, Pharaoh," said Moses. "The next plague is upon you. It's a plague of lice, cooties, and other tiny, itchy vermin. Now—let my people go."

"No," said Pharaoh, scratching.

"Next, the plague of flies!" said Moses. And God sent swarms of flies upon Pharaoh, his servants, and his people. And swarms of flies into their houses. And swarms of flies all over the ground so there was no place where there were no flies. And there was a tremendous buzzing in the land of Egypt. And still Pharaoh would not let his slaves go.

So Moses and Aaron said to him, "Let my people go or there will be another plague. This time it will be upon the live-stock. All the cows will be sick and unhealthy." And that is what happened to all the cows and livestock in Egypt except in the land of Goshen where the Children of Israel lived.

And Pharaoh said, "Okay, okay. I'll let your people go.
But get rid of these frogs."

However, Pharaoh was not impressed and his answer was still, "No!"

So Moses and Aaron said, "This time it's boils, Pharaoh. Please, let my people go."

And all the Egyptians got boils on their bodies. They were so bad, nobody could stand up or walk or anything. But Pharaoh said, "No!" and that rhymes with mo' and that's what he got. Mo' and mo'.

Moses announced the next plague. "A hailstorm," he said. "Hail to the Chief!"

And the Lord sent thunder and hail and fire that ran along the ground. And it was very grievous and there had never been anything like it in all the time Egypt had been a country. It broke everything it fell on—houses, trees, people, everything.

"This is enough," pleaded Pharaoh. "I pray to the Lord that there be no more of this. My goodness, you're breaking my heart. You're turning Pharaohland into Pharaoh's folly."

The hail stopped, so Pharaoh said, "I changed my mind. It's a Pharaoh's prerogative."

Moses said, "A plague of locusts, Pharaoh. To cover everything and eat every green thing and make the land barren."

The locusts came and lived up to their advance publicity and then some, but Pharaoh, who was definitely a stubborn man, said, "No!"

Moses said then, "A thick darkness over the land that will last for three days. And no one will see anything. This is a BIG DARKNESS. This is TOTAL DARKNESS. 100 percent zip visibility."

And the darkness descended upon the land and for three days no one could see anyone or anything, and it was terrible and this time Pharaoh was impressed.

"Now you got me angry," he told Moses. "Get out of my Royal presence. If I ever see your face again, you shall die. I'll never give in. Ever. Under any circumstances." Moses was banished.

"What's next?" he asked God.

And God replied, "One more plague and one more thing. Tell the Israelites to ask the Egyptians to lend them their jewels of gold and silver."

Moses said, "I don't know if we'll be able to pay them back. I guess we'll just consider the jewels as payment for years of slavery; and, who knows, it might come in handy to have negotiable gold and silver while we are traveling."

God spoke, "The last plague will be terrible. At midnight, I will go out into the midst of Egypt and all the firstborn in the land of Egypt shall die, from the firstborn of the Pharaoh to the firstborn of his servants and his animals."

Moses bowed his head. "That will surely convince him," he said. "That's an ultimate."

And that is what God did, but the Children of Israel were saved and the way they were spared is what Passover means.

On the night in which every firstborn should die, God had instructed the Children of Israel to kill a lamb and paint some of the lamb's blood on the sides of the door and above it. That would be a sign to the Lord to *pass over* (get it?) that house and spare those inside: the Children of Israel.

[41]

They left in an awful hurry—can you blame them?

And he told them to roast the lamb and eat it that night with bitter herbs. And eat it dressed and ready for a journey. Not the lamb dressed and ready for a journey, but the Children of Israel—*they* were to be dressed and ready for a journey.

That night, when God's hand passed through Egypt and took the lives of every firstborn, there went up a horrible cry from every house. There was terrible suffering in the land of Egypt and then Pharaoh sent the Children of Israel out from the land of Egypt.

They left in an awful hurry—can you blame them?—and so they had to take off with their bread still in the pans. That bread never rose like bread is supposed to, and turned into matzohs—the very first matzohs. The Children of Israel rose to the occasion, but the bread didn't.

And there were 600,000 men, not counting women and children, who left Egypt that night.

Samson and Delilah

Samson, the strong man, was one of the truly great dummies of the Old Testament. His story is found in the Bible in the Book of Judges. It begins in Chapter 13, if you really want to know, and goes on from there.

Samson was a charmed person. In fact, before he was born, an Angel of the Lord came down and first told his mother she was going to have a baby—a strong baby, a *very* strong baby, a super strong baby—and second gave her a very specific instruction about the baby. It was: "Don't let him have his hair cut, ever, because God intends him to use his strength against the Philistines and the secret of his strength is in his hair, and if anyone should cut his hair, he will lose his power for sure."

Samson's people, the Israelites, had been living under the rule of the Philistines for forty years at this time, and they were most uncomfortable because the Philistines were awful and rotten and mean and didn't appreciate anything. They just liked to go around and break things. And even today, if you come across anybody who fits that description, you can call him or her a Philistine. On second thought, maybe you shouldn't, they might break you.

As a child, Samson was the strongest boy in the neighborhood. The other kids worked out, did push-ups, chin-ups, ate the right things, drank their milk—all of it—the whole enchilada. However, no matter what they did, they just couldn't match Samson for strength. And besides that, he had never cut his hair or let anyone touch his hair. He was very touchy about his hair.

"Don't touch my hair. Get away from my hair," he warned anyone who came too close.

Staying away from Samson's hair posed some difficulty, inasmuch as there was so much of it. It was all over the place, even when combed.

When he walked down the street, people flattened themselves against the wall on both sides of the street in order to avoid his hair.

When he went to a sporting event and took his seat, no one sat behind him for three rows for fear of coming in contact with his hair and incurring his wrath. And besides, who could see?

The other boys and girls wanted to call him Samson the Hairball, but they were afraid of him and called him Samson the Mighty instead.

As he grew into manhood, the legend of his fabulous

He was so strong he could uproot trees with one hand,
break bricks with another.

strength and of his hairy deeds spread everywhere. He was so strong he could uproot trees with one hand, break bricks with the other. And once, when he was riled, he slew a thousand Philistines with the jawbone of an ass as his weapon.

That's the background on Samson, but now it's time to get to the meat of the story and ask the question: Can a man with a lot of hair and not much sense find happiness with an untrustworthy woman? And the answer to that is: Not if she's working for the Philistines. Every Achilles has his heel and Samson had his Delilah.

Delilah was Samson's girl friend. She was quite lovely. He thought the world of her. He just adored her. She was so cute and she was so good to him.

She peeled his grapes and gave him hot cocoa with a big marshmallow in it and always kept a large supply of cookies and cakes on hand. His favorite foods.

One day when Samson wasn't there the five rulers of the Philistines came to see Delilah and said to her, "We have to get Samson. He's too strong for us. Entice him, and see what it is that makes him so strong so we can catch him."

She said, "Samson's a lot of man."

They said, "Here's a lot of money."

She said, "It's a deal."

And there you have it, Samson, bought and sold and yet to be delivered.

So the sly Delilah started to play this not-so-clever game with the not-so-clever Samson. It was known as the Samson and Delilah Game and Samson, trusting fool that he was, loved it because it was all about him.

She asked him, "What is the secret of your great strength?"

And he told her something stupid. "Bind me with seven new bowstrings and I'll be as weak as a kitten."

She did and he stood there and said, "I feel as weak as a kitten."

Then she said, to test him, "Samson, the Philistines are here."

"What?" he said, breaking his bonds and flexing his muscles.

A cloud passed over Delilah's pretty face. She knew then that Samson had not told her the truth. She knew then that she knew not the secret of his strength.

She tried again. And they played a few more versions of that game, to no avail. Delilah kept serving and wasn't making any points.

Time for a change of tactics, she thought, grinding out her cigarette in a box of chocolates. When the going gets tough, the tough get going, and this Samson's a hard nut.

"You said you loved me," she nagged. "You really said you loved me. How can you say you love me when you won't tell me something as simple as that?" She nagged and nagged and nagged.

"If you cared, if you truly cared, if you ever thought about me on your own—without my having to bring it up first—you'd tell me," she explained.

Samson never smelled a rat. But her nagging began to wear on him.

"Tell me, tell me, tell me," she kept saying.

"I can't, I can't, I can't," he answered.

When Samson finally awoke, there was a big surprise in store for him.

"Tell me, tell me, tell me," she said.

"I can't, I mustn't, I shouldn't," he answered.

"Tell me, tell me, tell me," she said.

"All right, I'll tell you," he said. "You see this hair. . . ."

"How can I help it?" she said.

"It's never been cut," he explained. "And if it were ever to be cut, I would become weak as, and be like, any other man."

"Wouldn't you like to take a nap while I send out for a barber's chair?" Delilah quickly said.

Samson, at this point not his smartest, did as she told him. And while he slept, Delilah called the barber.

The barber came in, and he and Delilah set to work. They cut and they hacked and they cut and they hacked and they cut and they hacked, and Samson slept peacefully.

"Careful, don't wake him," said Delilah.

"Don't worry," said the barber, "I'm nowhere near him yet."

He and Delilah worked far into the night and the barber was on time-and-a-half and a dinner allowance and into double time before they finished.

And while cutting Samson's hair they found in it a bird's nest with a family of robins, several old combs and brushes, a branch from an elm tree, a lost puppy, three bottles of milk, a small hammer, and two dozen long-stemmed roses.

When Samson finally awoke, there was a big surprise in store for him.

"Whogh," he said. "I feel weak. Oh! My hair. What's become of my hair?"

"Well," said Delilah, "that's life—hair today, gone tomorrow."

"How could you?" he said.

"I wanted to see your ears," she said, popping a chocolate into her pretty mouth.

And then the Philistines came and took him away and threw him in a cell and, since they were a pretty rotten bunch, they blinded him too—just to add injury to injury.

"Woe is me," said Samson. "I am just a shadow of my former self."

And they made him a slave. And he did labor in the prison house, which was in Gaza.

"Oh, woe is me," he said. "Here I am eyeless in Gaza."

But his hair began to grow. One thing about hair, it grows. And it grows.

"Oh, woe is me," Samson said. "I'm just a five o'clock shadow of my former self."

And as his hair returned so too did his strength. But for the first time Samson was smart and kept his mouth shut and waited for the moment, and the moment came.

The Philistines were celebrating the festival of Dagon, their god, in their great temple. And they thought it would be fun to have Samson there so they could laugh at him.

The Philistines had a low sense of entertainment. Their idea of a show, which they applauded and laughed at, was to put a grapefruit rind on Samson's head. Then someone took it off and substituted a cantaloupe. The audience went bananas, so they put a banana peel on his head.

"This is garbage," said Samson.

Then they set him between the pillars that supported the temple and laughed at him some more. And there were more than three thousand Philistines laughing.

But Samson didn't care. He prayed to God. "Oh, Lord, remember me, I pray thee, and strengthen me, I pray thee, only this once, oh God, that I may at once be avenged of the Philistines for my two eyes."

And with that, he grabbed the two pillars, one with his right hand and one with his left, and said, "Let me die like an old trouper," and brought the house down.

And the house fell upon all the lords, and upon all the people that were in it, and they died.

So that was Samson. And the Bible says that the Philistines that he slew at his death were more than they which he slew in his life. And the moral of the story is, don't pick bad friends, they'll only get you in trouble. And another thing you might notice about this story is that, even though Samson was tricked and even though he wasn't working at it, he was still an instrument of the Lord against the Philistines, just as the Angel had predicted.

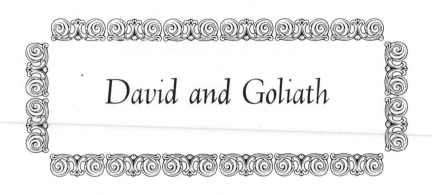

David and Goliath

The story of David and Goliath is in the Old Testament, the First Book of Samuel, Chapter 17. It's a story of the large and the heavy and the small and the crafty. The high and the mighty and the lowly and the humble. The tall and the short and the light and the dark. And the sweet and the sour. You might call it a story of contrast.

When our story begins, the Army of the Children of Israel has been challenged by the Army of the Philistines. It is a time of war. The Philistines were terrible people, who hated anything nice like Art or Poetry or Music. And they had no taste. For breakfast they had a glass of grease; for lunch, a bowl of grease; and for dinner, a dish of grease. If they were greasy, it was no coincidence. And their champion, Goliath, was every inch a Philistine and a greaseball—all 114 inches of him—that's nine and a half feet tall—that's a giant. That's a monster!

And he was a mess. His uniform was a mess. His tent was a mess. And he didn't make his bed, he swept it—and not too often. That was because sometimes he would have dinner in bed, fall asleep, and roll in his dinner. His bed got to be so greasy that some nights he would get into it and slide right out.

Goliath was heart and soul and body and mind a Philistine. He stood for everything they did. Every day he would get up and say, "When I get my hands on a good book, I just can't put it down. Get me a classic. Watch me tear right through it."

And every day he tore a book into teeny, weeny, weeny pieces with his bare hands.

And when he was through with his office work, he went out to taunt the soldiers of the Children of Israel. He did that every day, twice a day. He liked to stand on a high hill and look down on them and yell:

"Hey, you guys over there. You want to learn the truth about yourselves . . . you'd rather twitch than fight."

"Give me some men who are stouthearted men, because all I see in front of me is a bunch of chickens. Here, chickie. Here, chickie. Yah, yah, yah."

And the soldiers of the Children of Israel would boo him, "Boooooooooooooo!"

And he would go on.

"Can't take it, huh? There's more where that came from. You think you're so strong? I've seen better mussels in a fish store."

To which they replied, "Booooooo! That stinks!"

To which he replied, "Your mother wears Army sandals!"

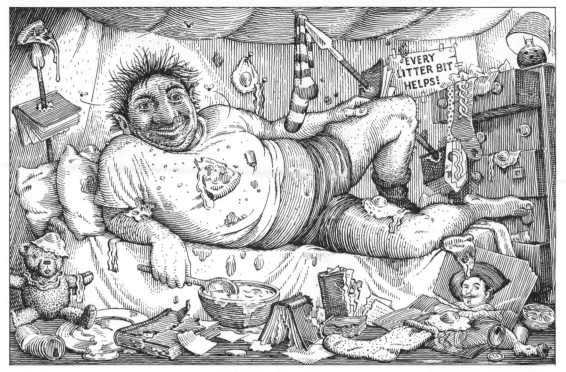

Goliath was a mess.

David was handsome. He was gifted. He played the lute
and the lyre, and he sang in the choir.

To which they replied, "Get a writer!"

To which he replied, "Your father wears a girdle."

To which they replied, "Lord deliver us!"

He liked to cap off his performance with a rendition of "Look at you, the hoo hoo with the ha ha on your head. Which of you wants to fight? Come on—yah, yah, yah!"

Of course no one came forward to fight Goliath. No one in his right mind would. Goliath was a beast.

And now for a change of pace, we shift our scene to David, the young shepherd, high on a lonely hill. David was one of the civilians of the Children of Israel. David was everything you wanted in a person. He was handsome. He was gifted. He played the lute and the lyre, and he sang in the choir. And he had good taste.

One day, as he was playing on the lyre and singing to his sheep, he remembered his brothers at the front. He put down his lyre and he said, "Enough of this interlude. I have to do something for the war effort. I've got it! I'll go and entertain the boys and I'll pack my brothers a picnic basket of goodies. I'll bring them some lovely cheese—some camembert, some brie, some tilsit . . . and some splendid wine."

He sniffed some wine and put it into the basket along with the cheeses. "This one has a nice bouquet," he said. "And now to the front," he said as he moved off.

Well, when he got there, Goliath was still at his usual spot, mouthing off, just as he had been for forty days. As David came nearer, he could hear Goliath.

"As an army you ought to go far . . . soon. And I hope you stay there."

"Take my life . . . please."

"You guys are one for the books. The Book of Dumbbells."

And so bad were these jokes that the Children of Israel rolled on the ground in deep agony and clutched their sides to keep from crying. One of them said to David, "Now you see why war is hell."

And David said, "This is terrible. This is the worst I've ever heard. Something's got to be done about this."

So David went to the Army of the Children of Israel Headquarters (the A.C.I.H.) to see his Commander-in-Chief, King Saul.

Saul said, "Sit down, Dave, I'll be with you in a minute. This Goliath business has got me down. I've got the three Ds. I'm Disheartened, Dismayed, and Depressed."

And David said, "Hold on! I've got two Hs. High Hopes."

Saul then posed the question, "Does a Shepherd with 2 Hs beat a King with 3 Ds?"

David replied, "Yes. Cheer up, King Saul, I'm going to challenge Goliath."

Saul was not as optimistic as David.

He said, "You? Why this armor alone weighs twice as much as you do. What makes you think you can go out there and face a giant like Goliath and live to keep your place in history? I see great things for you. Why come a cropper with a creep like Goliath?"

But David answered, "If I come a cropper, that'll be my share. I'll be a sharecropper. However, I don't think I will, because our God is on my side."

Then Saul offered him his own personal armor-plated armor.

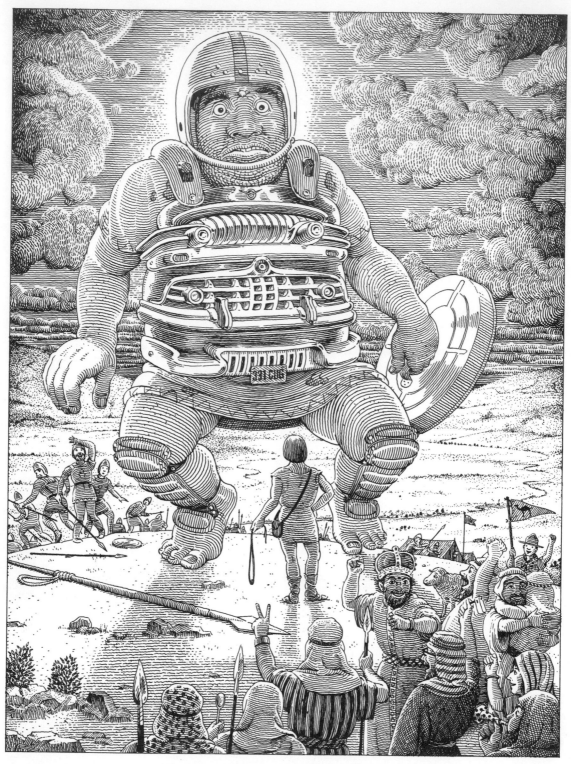

The stone sank into Goliath's forehead.

"Well, if you put it that way," Saul said, "go ahead. But take my armor . . . please."

David shook his head and turned it down, saying delicately, "No thank you. It's too baroque. I've got my slingshot and five smooth stones. My motto is: Less is more."

So David, the Aesthete, met Goliath, the Philistine, on the Field of Battle. And when David got there, Goliath was in rare form. He was killing the crowd with his jokes, laying 'em dead in the aisles.

"You guys are so short, you put your feet in your pockets and walk on your hands."

"You guys are so weak, it takes two of you to breathe."

And the Children of Israel were saying to him, "Get outta here! Take a bus!"

To which Goliath threw back, "Why don't you take a long walk off a short pier?"

"Why don't you leave me alone and go play in the traffic?"

"Why don't you put yourself in an envelope and mail it?"

"Why don't you put an egg in your shoe and beat it? Scram bola!"

Just then David interrupted him, "Goliath, yoo hoo. I've come to take your challenge."

Goliath looked around and didn't see anybody. That was because Goliath was so tall and David was so small.

So David called out again, "Yoo hoo. Down here, Goliath."

Goliath found him after a while. And was he surprised!

"You?" he said. "You? You are going to challenge *me*? That's the funniest thing I ever heard."

He started to laugh. "You're so little," he said, falling to his knees and pounding the ground.

He laughed so hard, tears popped out of his eyes, and when he beat on the ground, it shook so much, David was bounced in the air.

But David was starting to boil.

"Get up and fight like a man," he told Goliath.

Goliath stood up. He fixed David with the business end of his steely glare and spat out the following statement:

"Sure, little flea. But I'm warning you right now, I'm going to make bird food and cat meat out of you."

He pulled out his sword.

"Where's your weapon?" he asked.

David told him, "I have a leather sling and five stones and one of them has your name on it."

Goliath defied him, "Oh, yeah? Let me have it."

"Okay," said David, "you asked for it."

And David put his hand in his bag and pulled out a stone, inserted it into his sling, swung the sling three times over his head, and slung the stone. The stone sank into Goliath's forehead and he fell upon his face to the earth. Stone dead.

And after that David took Goliath's sword and cut off Goliath's head. And then he showed it to everybody.

And that is the story of how David rocked Goliath to sleep, permanently.

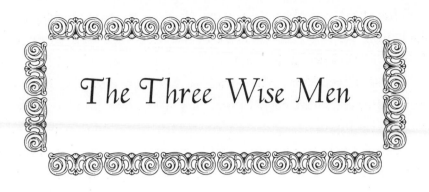

The Three Wise Men

The birth of Christ in the Little Town of Bethlehem a long time ago was more than just a local news story. Even then it was an international event, and the proof of that was the coming of the Three Wise Men from the East. There's a story about them and a holiday for them, and that's called Epiphany. Epiphany is traditionally celebrated on January 6. Their story—if you want to look it up—is found in Chapter 2 of Matthew in the New Testament.

Now let's get on to the story of the Three Wise Men. First of all the three of them were Kings, and their names were: Melchior, Gaspar, and Balthazar.

Melchior came from Arabia. He was the oldest and had a flowing white beard and white hair, and he was very smart.

Gaspar, the King of Tarsus, was the youngest. He had red hair on top of his head and he was very bright.

The third member of the party was Balthazar. He was a black man with a bushy, black beard, and he came from Saba. He was very knowledgeable.

These Three Wise Men, each in his own country, hundreds of miles apart from each other, saw a strange and very bright star in the heavens, and that meant to them that a new King was being born somewhere. So they each set out by camel to follow the star in order to find this new King and worship him.

Because they were following the same star, they eventually met on the road and joined forces and traveled together, always following the star. This meant that they had to travel at night, and when a cloud covered the star, they just had to wait until it passed.

The star finally led them to the city of Jerusalem, in the land of the Jews, which was ruled by King Herod. It is said that Herod called his niece Salome, Salami, because he had a rye sense of humor. He, in turn, was known as the Wry King, a snappy cracker. He was also vain and evil—what you would call a bad combination. Unlike the Three Wise Men, who were Kings, Herod was a King who was not wise.

When Herod heard about the Three Wise Men who were asking around, "Where is he that is born King of the Jews?" he was disturbed.

"I've been hearing talk of a new King," he told his scribes, "and I'm disturbed—I've been disturbed for a long time, but this really disturbs me. One country—one King, that's the rule. One King to a country. Our national motto is: All for one, and one for one, and I'm the one. I want you to explain this new King business to me."

Herod suddenly turned to Gaspar and said,
"That's a cute pair of shoes you got there."

And his scribes answered, "There is a prophecy that out of Bethlehem shall come a King that shall rule the People of Israel."

"Enough!" shouted Herod. "Bring me the Three Wise Men. I'll get to the bottom of this."

So the Three Wise Men were brought before Herod. "Tell me about this star you've been following. When did you first see it?" he asked them.

The Three Wise Men answered, "We come from the East. We each saw this very bright star and it led us here."

"I see," said Herod, who suddenly turned to Gaspar and asked, "That's a cute pair of shoes you got there. I like the curly toes. Where'd you get them?"

"Ahmad, the shoemaker; they're on special—only thirty-one drachmas," replied Gaspar.

"Smiley," called Herod to one of his flunkies, "order me two pairs in Blue, 8½ triple E." Then he turned back to the Three Wise Men. "My scribes tell me that you've come to the wrong place," he told them. "My scribes tell me that it's going to happen in the Little Town of Bethlehem. My scribes tell me that it is written that such a thing will come to pass. But what do they know, anyway?"

"Wherever the star leads us, that's where we'll follow," the Three Wise Men told him. "If it takes us to the Little Town of Bethlehem, so be it. That's where we'll go."

"You do that," said Herod. "Go and search diligently for the young child, and when you have found him, bring me word again, that I may come and worship him also."

"Thank you very much," answered the Three Wise Men, bowing and walking backwards out of the King's chambers. "We'll be going now. Good-bye. And we hope you enjoy your shoes."

After they had gone, Herod told his scribes, "I was going to send a legion of soldiers to search for the Infant King so I could kill him, but now they'll find him for me."

This was evidence that Herod was not 100 percent in the think department, nor was he 80 or 60 or 40 percent, no, try 20 or 25 percent, and you'd be closer to the truth, because even the dimmest noo-noo brain in the kingdom could have figured out that the star was there for everyone to see and anyone could follow it, not just the Three Wise Men. And, for that matter, Herod could have gone out and followed the Three Wise Men himself. But Herod's mind was so much on those shoes that he had to stay home and wait for them.

The Three Wise Men followed the star, and lo and behold it did take them to Bethlehem, and it went before them till it came and stood over where the young child was, in a stable, wrapped in swaddling clothes and lying in a manger, because there was no room at the inn.

And although the surroundings were humble, the Three Wise Men rejoiced with exceeding great joy. "Hello, Mary and Joseph and Lord Baby Jesus," they said, "we are Three Wise Men, sometimes we're called Magi and sometimes we're called Kings, and we've come a great distance following that yonder star to bring you these gifts."

The Three Wise Men rejoiced with exceeding great joy.

And then they sang:

"We three Kings of Orient are.
  Bearing gifts we traverse afar.
  Field and fountain, moor and mountain,
  Following yonder star.
  Oh, star of wonder, star of might,
    Star with royal beauty bright,
  Westward leading, still proceeding,
    Guide us to the perfect light."

After the song, Melchior announced, "Now for the gifts. Oh, you'll love these. I bring you gold to show that you are a King." And he gave the infant Jesus his gift of gold.

"I bring you frankincense to show that you are holy," said Gaspar, stepping forward and putting his gift at the baby's feet.

"And I bring myrrh," said Balthazar, kneeling, "because you are mortal."

The Lord Baby Jesus blessed them and they thanked him.

"Thank you, Lord Baby Jesus, we're going back now," they said, "to tell Herod and then the whole world that you were born."

And they mounted their camels and rode off in the direction of Herod's palace.

"I can hardly wait to tell Herod. Won't he be thrilled?" said Melchior.

"The King of the Jews is come," said Gaspar.

"The King of the Jews *has* come," corrected Balthazar, and they quickened their pace.

Suddenly they heard a noise, "Pssst!"

"What was that?" said Gaspar.

"Sounds like you're getting a flat," said Melchior.

"Don't be silly," said Balthazar, "he's riding a camel."

"Then it must be an angel," said Gaspar. "Whoa, Abdul!" he instructed his camel.

"Whoa, Abdul!" they all said to their camels, and their camels stopped.

And there above them, just to the right, standing on a small cloud, floating in the air, stood an angel—wings, halo, glowing robes, shimmering iridescence, the complete and total angel ensemble.

"Hold on there, Wise Men," said the angel. "I'm sent by the Lord to tell you not to go back to Jerusalem and see Herod. Just go and tell the world. Leave Herod alone. He's up to no good."

"Thank you for that message, Angel," the Three Wise Men told him. "We'll skip Herod and go directly to tell the world." And that's what they did.

The angel also appeared to Joseph and told him to take the Infant Jesus and Mary into Egypt and there to remain until Herod's death, so they would be safe from Herod's jealousy.

Meanwhile, back at the palace, Herod was sitting alone by the telephone.

"Where are those Three Wise Men?" he complained. "They said they'd be back and I'm waiting. They haven't called or anything. And my feet are killing me. Why did I let them talk me into buying those shoes?"

The Prodigal Son

The story of the Prodigal Son is in Chapter 15 of the Book of Luke in the New Testament, and it has to do with Jesus Christ. The Book of Luke tells us that Jesus, as he was going around as a preacher, spoke to everyone and anyone. And he would sit down and break bread—that is, have dinner—with known sinners. But the Pharisees and the Scribes, who were the important people in the community and the upright, up-tight people in the community, didn't like this, and they said to him,

"You eat with sinners, Jesus. You waste your time with hooligans and ruffians—lowlifes—you're a finer sort. You could be hanging around with a better class of people. You could join the country club."

And Jesus answered them by telling a parable. A parable is a story that you make up to illustrate the point you want to get across. And a parable is not two bulls in a field. Backwards it's elbarap, but that means nothing. So that's something you can forget. Remember that. Forget it.

The particular parable that Jesus told them is called the Prodigal Son. And the moral is: When a sinner repents, there is more joy in heaven than over ninety-nine just people who need no repentance. Now, see if the parable proves that point.

Once upon a time there was a farmer who had two sons. One was named Jack and one was named Rudy. Jack was the good one.

He would say things like, "Gee, I wish there was more work for me to do. I wish Dad would let me scrub the stables."

And he would mean it.

And the other son, Rudy, was the Prodigal. Rudy had seen too many movies, watched too much television, and read too many racy books. His head was full of silly ideas of high living. He would say things like, "If I had a lotta money, man, I could have more fun, man. I could live, man. This is Dullsville."

And he would mean it.

So one day, Rudy asked his Dad for his inheritance. He said, "Please, Dad, I got big things to do. I want to enjoy life before I'm old and gray like you. I want to laugh. I want to dance. I want to sing. I want to leap into the sun. I'm young. I still got my figger."

So his father gave Rudy a big sack of gold and said, "This is your fair share of the farm. That's all it comes to. I'm paying you off in full and now the rest belongs to Jack."

And he added, "You're making me very sad, Rudy. You're

breaking my heart. I hate to see you like this. I hate to see you become . . . the Prodigal Son."

But Rudy wasn't listening because that's what he was. He was prodigal and profligate, in other words—a punk. And his money was burning a hole in his pocket and he had to get rid of it.

So he went to . . . the Big City. Also known as The Apple. He went directly to the first store he found that sold FLASHY CLOTHING! And he said to the clerk, "I got heat in my pockets, this money's burning holes. I got to spend it and spend it fast. Gimme a suit. I don't care how good it is, as long as it's expensive."

If you're the Prodigal Son, you got to look the part, he thought. Duds make the Dude.

And he got himself an outfit—a purple suit with brown pinstripes, eight-inch shoulder pads on the jacket, four-inch cuffs on the pants, contrasting gussets and plackets all around with piping, rickrack, and petit point. To complete the picture he got a pair of two tone wing-tip shoes and a hat with a feather in it He looked like two peacocks, back to back.

The next thing he needed was a place to hang his feathered hat. He decided to move into a hotel. He took a room at the Spitz.

"There's nothing like a room at the Spitz," he marveled. "It's where the hoi meets the polloi and riff meets raff. What class! Gosh, any night of the week you can meet salesmen in the lobby. And the luxury," he rejoiced. "You never have to make your bed. They bring you food anytime you ask for it.

"Let me have one of each flavor, please.
And double cones for the house. It's all on me!"

Anything. Candy bars, popcorn, chewing gum. My teeth are decaying, but I don't care. There's no Tomorrow. Only the Now!"

He wasted his days in riotous living. He went next door to the ice cream parlor often.

"Let me have one of each flavor, please. Don't scrimp on the sprinkles—I'm paying. And double cones for the house. It's all on me!" he would shout.

He was very popular with ice cream addicts.

Around the Spitz he was known for his tips.

"Bellhop, get me a new shoelace. Here's twenty cents for the lace and a fifty-dollar tip."

He was very popular with bellhops.

He took to gambling and went every day to the Casino Reno, sometimes known as the Reno Casino.

"Let the chips fall where they may. Ahhhhh, this is the life. Chance to have fun and lose everything I own. Who could ask for anything more?" he laughed.

Until one day he put his hand in his sack to take out another gold coin and the sack was empty.

"Uh oh," he said. "Where did it go? Whoops, moment of truth. That's one thing about money—when it's gone, it's gone. You know what I think, I think the bank broke me."

Out of money and out of luck, the Prodigal Son began the inevitable descent—the road down.

They threw him out of the Spitz because he couldn't pay his bill. And they kept his bags, which held all his earthly possessions. His suit got torn and he didn't look so good. In fact, he looked worse in his new torn suit than he had in his faded coveralls.

"These spiffy shoes don't look so good in the rain. The holes in my wing tips let the water in," he complained to no one in particular because no one in particular was listening. It was raining and the weather was foul. Rudy had lost all his fair-weather friends.

He continued his downward trip. In order to get money to eat, Rudy became the Poor Little Match Boy.

"Please buy my matches. Won't someone buy my matches?" he cried.

It snowed, and the wind howled all around him, and his clothes turned to rags, and the patches on his pants froze hard like little boards, and nobody bought his matches.

Rudy was rapidly descending. He was on an express elevator from the top to the bottom.

He had to find something else to do, but when he looked in the want ads for jobs, there were no job openings for Prodigal Sons. In fact, the ads read, "Prodigal Sons need not apply."

So poor Rudy went back to what he knew. He went to work for a farmer. A pig farmer.

"S–O–O–O–I–I–I–I!   S–O–O–O–I–I–I–I! Pig! Pig! Pig! Pig! Pig! Pig!" he hollered all day long. And he thought to himself, So here I am working for this pig farmer. But the job has some extras. I can eat the leftovers. I can have all the pig food the pigs don't eat.

Then he remembered something. Pigs don't leave no leftovers. "Oh, I'm so depressed," he wailed.

He started to cry and walk away, and he didn't look where he was going. Suddenly he felt something cold and mushy on his ankles, on his knees, on his thighs, on his waist, on his chest, up to his chin. He was down and sinking.

"This is Bottomsville," he said, up to his neck in mud. "I'm up to my neck in mud and no place to take a bath. I want to go home. I feel so broke up, I want to go home. I made a mistake. I've wasted my inheritance. I want to go home in the worst way and that's the way I'm going too," he said as he climbed out of the mud puddle.

Rudy started the Long Walk Home. As he walked along the road, he was covered in so much dirt that radishes and potatoes were growing all over him. He looked like a walking vegetable patch.

And he kept saying to himself, "Oh, I hope Jack and Poppa take me back. Or at least let me stay in the barn. Maybe I can ask them for a job. Maybe if I'm lucky they'll let me be a hired hand. Oh, I'm so sorry. Oh, if they only knew what I went through. Nobody knows the trouble I've seen. And all of it just to prove them right."

Then he saw it off in the distance. His father's farm! He started to run.

"Dad, Dad, it's me, Rudy! Forgive me. I've come home. Forgive me. I am not worthy to be your son. Daddy, I've been a meshugana!" he shouted.

And his father answered, "Is that you, Rudy? Rudy? Is that you? Rudy, you look terrible, but I'm glad you're home."

And his father said to his servants, "My boy Rudy is back.

"Is that you, Rudy? Rudy? Is that you?
You look terrible, but I'm glad you're home."

The apple of my eyeball. Bring clothes for his back, shoes for his feet, and a ring for his finger. Bring hither the fatted calf, kill it, and let us eat and be merry, for Rudy is back. He has learned his lesson. And somebody, please, give him a bath."

So Rudy was back on the farm. There was a big celebration for him, and he sat at the head of the table stuffing himself on fatted calf. He told everyone who would listen, "Gosh, it's good to be home!"

But how did Jack feel about all this? Well, this is what he said: "I'm really not too pleased. Rudy took his inheritance, ran off, had a good time, spent everything, and when he didn't have anything left, he came back here, and look at the reception you gave him. I've been here the whole time and nobody's ever given me a party."

And his father replied, "Look at it this way, Jack. Rudy didn't have such a good time of it. And he's really sorry now. Besides that, he's spent his inheritance and you've got everything. You've got it all. The moral of this story is, Jack, that when someone's truly repentant and sorry for what he did, don't close the door on him, rejoice."

And Jack said, "I guess you're right. Well, I got to go harvest my crops. I got to go tend to my land. I got to wash a field and polish a meadow. And maybe I'll feed a pair of bulls."

And that is the story of Rudy, the Prodigal Son, and Jack, the Good Son.

Afterword

Good-night, King James, wherever you are.

As Marshall Efron and Alfa-Betty Olsen point out in their foreword, the idea for this book came from their CBS television program, "Marshall Efron's Illustrated, Simplified and Painless Sunday School" in which Marshall was the sole performer and which they both wrote. The show received both critical acclaim and the approval of the National Council of the Churches of Christ in the U.S.A. This is their first book. Up until now most of their work, singly and together, has been in television, theater, or motion pictures. They both live in Greenwich Village because they don't like city life.

Ron Barrett is the illustrator of a number of picture books, including *Benjamin's 365 Birthdays* (Atheneum), which was a Children's Book Showcase selection. He is a former advertising art director turned editor for *The Electric Company Magazine* published by the Children's Television Workshop. He says that he had a religious bent when growing up, as he came from ecumenical parentage—a Jewish mother and a Catholic father. "I shopped around for a religion. I went to different churches and synagogues and I read the Bible a lot. I listened to radio evangelists and once I almost became a Catholic by mail. When this manuscript dropped through the mail slot, my religious sensibilities were reawakened. Not only was it religious, but fun, too, with all of the magic left in."